The Last Tape

The Last Tape

Alex Niven

Winchester, UK
Washington, USA

First published by Zero Books, 2014
Zero Books is an imprint of John Hunt Publishing Ltd., Laurel House, Station Approach,
Alresford, Hants, SO24 9JH, UK
office1@jhpbooks.net
www.johnhuntpublishing.com
www.zero-books.net

For distributor details and how to order please visit the 'Ordering' section on our website.

Text copyright: Alex Niven 2013

ISBN: 978 1 78279 545 2

A CIP catalogue record for this book is available from the British Library.

Design: Lee Nash

Printed in the USA by Edwards Brothers Malloy

We operate a distinctive and ethical publishing philosophy in all
areas of our business, from our global network of authors to
production and worldwide distribution.

CONTENTS

In the borderland, up on Hartside Fell,
There is an old abandoned well;
I came upon it, cold and lost,
Wandering through the northern frost.

Wandering through the frost and rain
The storm of life drove through my brain;
Taking shelter from the wet
I chanced upon this old cassette.

1.

One of these days there will be movement

WINNING

A gang of us at first, breaking
into the mildewed football ground
hours before dawn, scouring
the lime white terraces for an apt
space to launch from, the concrete
like the surface of the moon.
In the powerful light of this
in between place you see faces as if
for the first time – stars, glances –
the chinks in the cantilever stand
allow some small rays to filter through.
We don't know what we're doing.
There are risings in the east we think
must come stammering into life;
we will die for kinship or fail
forever in our sniggering selves.
Here lies the largest congregation
in the western world. Miles above
the paving stones, scintillating
the leaves, our flares reignite the sky.

1989

They came swooshing like water
out of Leppings Lane, leaping
into the matchday sun. Soon
bodies ghosted the gym.

All I dreamt of back then were
vague summaries of light, now
nightmares of black hammers
pummelling the helpless.

THE DOMINICAN FRIARS COME TO ENGLAND

We set the country alight.
Miracles in the marketplace
and tales of the pure earth.
Girl gaggles followed us.

They were a susceptible people
and we were young, skint.
Peacock parading
was our schoolboy itch.

Anyway, we meant it
at that juncture.
We were trying to scatter
rainbows,

poetry, anything.
You can't imagine
the blue-veined love
I had for the world, back then.

Dreams stacked up.
Dogs gambolled with us.
We felt that our convoy would
lead to Lyonesse.

By Michaelmas we
were fat as bullocks,
and the pennants of the new
true life glazed the hills.

Just out of sight
the Mother Church
was clucking her teeth.
She must have known all along.

HIDDEN TRACK

I couldn't work out whether
you were part of the future
or a beautiful aftershock.

Blind spots where the sun snuck.
Your skin was syncopated, weightless.
We crossed every finish line,
woke immaculately new.

REMEMBRANCE DAYS

We seem unable to move on.
                              Beached fish
say forever is a butterfly life.
A studio reel-to-reel oiled smooth, safe.

(Photos clacker past, watermarks vanish.)

Dawn autumns the dust choked village hall.
                                        Curled
beneath the hymnbooks and the nursery chairs
a spider spins the first new form in years.

We surge, we gather, in another world.

PANTISOCRACY

We were barracked in a lonely ranch.
Food sacks for the winter.
Salt.
Inured to the pulse of things.

Leaving the coastal towns was hard.
We left trinkets.
Warriors were expunged
from the phonebook.

But then, the ranch-lands glittered.
Banquets scarfed by the hearth.
Green wet grass everywhere
goading us.

My sweetheart fished for salmon.
I sang.
Friends delivered the basic mete
and railroads arrived latterly.

Only, something had broken.
For hours we battered the bonnet
mad for the snag
eyes freezing at the rim.

Now the fells loomed and burgeoned.
Friends withered and sank.
Heart-stuck
you loved the flickering silver ash.

In the mist one Monday
I began walking. They found me
knee-deep in the tarn
weeping at the space between cities.

THE EXILE OF DELIA DERBYSHIRE

Twelve miles south of the border
In a farmhouse empty of sound,
I ply my ambient trade,
Cutting tape, carving the wind.

In the sixties at flower-filled parties,
Those echoing scales in the air;
In the sixties at flower-filled parties,
In my Quant gown and my bobbed hair.

Now I drink glasses of bitter
In Cumbrian workingmen's bars:
Playing darts, fading into the margins,
Flutter of wind in my ears.

PLAYBOY OF THE WESTERN WORLD

His face a sallow desiccated pitch,
moonscape of booze-ruin and suffering,
Paul Gascoigne sits amid the staggered crowd
of black and white as we go down
2-0 to Chelsea (which is probably
the death of us this year, to tell the truth),
a camera pausing on his look of dog
despair, his quake-like elemental sigh.
And I remember stepping on his heels
one day when he was only twenty-three,
a gaggle of us kids clung on, entranced
by this heroic figure gliding through
a guest appearance signing photographs
at Dunston Federation Brewery.

THE LAST BHUNDU BOY

In a coffee shop down by the Water of Leith
He speaks of the death of the band,
Killing time for a bored *Daily Record* reporter –
Website feature, cash in hand.

He tells of the legendary home-taping eighties
When African boys were in vogue;
He tells of the transient headlining highlife
And the legendary man-eating plague.

Back in the Special-Brew damp of the hostel
He weeps at the death of the band,
And the breaking of every fellowship
In this desolate post-eighties land.

ON THE PROPOSED RENAMING OF ST JAMES'S PARK

"Apparently it was a turtle massacre"

Let this
be a lesson
to you:
names
don't matter!
Remember
Shakespeare,
Saussure,
think of
Derrida.

Meaning slips
and slides,
is not
fascistic,
cannot
be controlled,
has
no memory,
soon runs
out of juice;

see this
wagon full of
terrapins
stalling and
then
failing
in a final
abject disaster
halfway down
the A69.

ON THE FOOTBRIDGE OVER THE A12 AT LEYTONSTONE

The Shard spears clouds.

> The day we moved here
> a beautiful girl of sixteen
> slid over the railing
> into the traffic bleeding
> northwards out of this suicide city.

London glitters in nooks.

> But isn't everyone always
> running aground in the glare
> of those sky limned towers,
> those men who will not dim
> their lights for the love of money?

CHARLOTTE WITHERS

We might have fallen quite melodiously in love.

Her father
the widowed Mr. Withers
was in town visiting his umquwhile clientage
on carboniferous business.

While he wandered
on the coal wharves
we disputed the relative merits
of painting and music;
I wrote an essay nine foolscap pages long
dedicated to the total overthrow
and discomfiture of her opinions
and the establishment of mine.

She wasn't pretty
rather: pleasant
in a wild-flower sort of way
especially if her eyes were looking at you
and her mind with them.

I said goodbye
to this fragile, freckled,
fair, sensitive slip of a girl
on Camberwell Green in the Spring of '38.

A short while later
her father "negotiated" her marriage
to a Newcastle coal merchant
who treated her pretty much as one of his coal sacks
and she died within the year.

(Ruskin, *Praeterita*, pp. 207-8.)

WHAT SOCIALIST LONDON WOULD LOOK LIKE

Not perfect of course, but better.

▶ ‖

One of these days   there will be movement

religion will return
      debt will   diminish
         dryads will writhe
    in the foreground
           forever

but today I hit pause   on your HC2 teeth
     your evolutionary hair
        your willingness
    to shrug away
       the universe
          for an unmarketable   instant

BRITISH POETRY 2010s

Every poem in this issue
took our breath away.
We're thrilled to be here.

Moil, voiceless, tendrils.
Frail bird-wings and The Body.
A healthy respect for form or

free verse for minimal cool.
CVs, junkets,
status-obsessives, word-molesters.

A sallow child
begging in the belly of power
for a bone.

NEW YORK POEMS

i.

Today I simmer
with afterthoughts,
addenda, bits
of notes and besides
you tell me
there is nothing
under the moon
we cannot undermine.

ii.

Curt islands, and
glass glimmering.
Wrist spangled.

Crushed men.

Another step and we're
back into the light.

iii.

Your eyes
are flayed with
the world's edge

and the chance
to be born all
over again.

iv.

birds giggle you

when fluttering boast
of your feathers

scythes sinew

it ghosts
my heart up

through

the shivering cup
of the sky

V.

my sentiments are
snowflakes

caught in the teeth
of a hairdryer

vi.

Right now there is no one.
The clerks are tearing down the towns.
The poor curdle in bunkers.
Records loop endlessly.

EPITAPH: NOUGHTIES POP

31/12/09

In sum, this decade offered up a flat
and absolute rebuttal to the notion that
the pop song is as literate as books:
The Killers, Razorlight, Snow Patrol, Muse, The Kooks.

THE BEEHIVE

*... one of the younger fellows, Howard Colvin ... believed that the
new project demanded a "frankly contemporary treatment which
would make no concessions to the adjoining buildings except in such
matters as scale and material".*
- Geoffrey Tyack, *Modern Architecture in an Oxford College 1945 -
2005*

We wanted something new. You see
there was a kind of playschool
surety back then: every degree
counted, every man could rule
a line back to the source, and spin
the other way and see it shoot
in fractal patterns out of his ken,
upending the official route.
We wanted something new, and we
would sacrifice most anything
(well, *decorum* definitely)
to get our gawky, sky-jostling
ruck with nature set in knifey
Portland stone. Of course, I know
time hasn't widened out the way
we reckoned all those years ago.
You plan for that, allow for that.
I know the building might have housed
the odd careerist democrat
or two, and yes, we missed
our chance to make a truly ideal
hive, a fair organic whole.
That too was calculable.
Facts played their usual role.

What niggles like a buzzing clock
are certain ambling sightseers,
how they so leisurely mock
our bid to level with the stars,
how smiling artisans can stare
me dead in the eye, ecstatically
perplexed when I say *future*.
We wanted something new, you see.

'The Beehive' St John's College, Oxford 1960

GALILEO

You get older and the roar starts

the void   flourishes
      you wonder   where the crowd went.

A cause to canvas for?

I wake up in the morning.
      It takes me hours   to focus

but when I manage it
      I stir slowly   rigged
          with a sort of ease   mindful

      of the Galilean orbits
         the way the sun splinters

     tracks   in the nightly snow

2.

a beat without pace

CHILLINGHAM CATTLE

Underneath the dancing stars
They walked with pale grace,
In the time before the world began
To a beat without pace.

From the North Sea to the foaming Clyde
They roamed through waves of trees,
The sun wept on their ancient hide,
The moon brokered their peace.

They lived and died a sacred herd,
They lived and grew as one,
The world beyond the dry stone walls
Grew fainter than the sun.

Later when the castled knights
Enclosed our common ground
They huddled in the heavy oaks,
Survived without sound.

Now in the light of the morning
They run from human hands,
The castled Duke is still the gaoler
Of these ancient lands.

Underneath the dancing stars
They wait with pale grace
For the waves to wash the world again,
For the untamed human face.

3.

In 2011 the revised Oxford English Dictionary announced that it would be removing the words "cassette tape" from its Concise version, causing some media backlash.

MEANING OF LIFE/VHS RENTAL

My first brush with death:
aged nine
I saw Daniel Day Lewis
in *Last of the Mohicans*.

It was the last day of
first school
and as the credits rolled
my eyes streamed.

So life is that … short,
and then you die?
Yes, said my dad,

but that is also what makes it
so
worthwhile.

CARTOONS

The land is a well-kept secret. From the row of houses lining the main road of the village the fields tumble greenly down to the river and then shoot back up to the top of the valley, a wide, world-shunning vista. Plantations of pines clumped against dry stone walls. Moors on the periphery, pillars of smoke in the distance. The train track follows the curve of the river as it severs the dale's green swathe gently in two, winding through the old station empty since they stopped digging limestone decades ago. Quarries hide in the woods on the hillsides, their last-hewn stones wound round with grass, conifers and craters where men once crowded to work.

A long, blank summer. I buried myself in the car panel warehouse, working 8 til 7, endless weeks, raw calves, hauling sumps, windscreens, bonnets. Black Monday mornings wilting in the sunless heat, pocketing small change, pointlessly stoic. Bowman, the village cartoon, fat cigar smoking capitalist, would wander down from his boss's layer, a tumoured warren, conservatories, protuberances, a gothic folly of the eighties. When he stooped behind us the air greyed over with greed, magnetised our last filaments of strength, his charcoal laugh the true sound of a century in which the old villainy is occulted but stoked, unabated.

At bait time we sat in an oil-stained hut. Jordan's breasts smiled at us from a faded poster, sun-worn diptych of the nineties. Those men hated that job, but they sat there for each other, trying to make jokes ring, finding ways to overlap, mostly agreeing. It was here that I saw paradise for the first time, in the arrangement of people, hatred of the residual cartoons, the proximity of minds. I think about the warehouse every day, though I rarely go back to the village, and some say it doesn't exist.

YEAR OUT

We packed body protectors
for horse riders.

I would say we were
saving lives, meanwhile

so many of those women
in the workroom

watched their dreams
disperse like

stray threads

out of broken
Singer machines.

NOTHING LIKE MY GHOST

I had miscarried
the year before

so this time
I was scared, adamant.

In the third month
Adam and June died.

The traffic police
chased their motorbike

til they battered
the bridge at Newbrough.

We sat in the cold church
and I paused my heart

stole into stone.
I would bulwark you.

It was a difficult birth
but when it was over

your dad paraded you
through the Terrace

like a football cup.
He was so proud.

Recomposed
I looked at your face

and felt a sudden
blind respect.

I couldn't believe
it was so equal

that you were whole,
another narrative

that you were nothing
like my ghost.

THE LAST TAPE

Crowds streamed along the path to the industrial estate.
There were rumours of spring, of oxygen.

We arrived at the waste disposal unit. A cargo of goods spilled
out of a storage container tied to a lorry.

Linoleum rolls, laptops, rabbit cages. Everything had rotted to
  mush.
A white polyester football shirt lay in the sun sighing with
  mould.

The crowd formed a circle. You came to me carrying an armful of
  rubbish.
The sun splashed ribbons of light over your beautiful hair.

After hours of waiting a cassette tape fell from the pile.
We shivered.

I kissed your mud-covered hands, and the music on the tape
spread and echoed through the crowd like holy thunder.

THE DANCE

Last night I dreamt
             our father came alive.
Crouched on a hilltop
             painted by Matisse
we listened to him say
             with phantom ease
that this nightmare was over.
             "You'll survive.
Son, get your driving licence passed.
             But I've
bled all the words I can.
             Forgive me, please,
you can't rewind
             the music of release.
Stop the reel. I have
             no strength to strive ..."

So then we wandered
             through the rainbow wood
following the trail
             of his remains;
and when I'd nearly
             given up the ghost
you led me through a sunshine copse
             we stood
upon a sprawling beach
             enclosed with chains
of families dancing
             all along the coast.

DAD'S FIRST WALKMAN

A grey wraith in a blue leather case,
Still a marvel in some respects:
Reminder of a sci-fi world,
Of buried futuristic sects.

After 1979
Our reeling hopes were all erased,
But the last tape can be wiped again
And the dreaming past can be rephrased.

NORTH SEA TRAVELOGUE

Exhausted, feeling hemmed in,
I took the first northbound train.
Making notes in a moleskine pad
I wrote down everything good I had:
girlfriend, sister, one or two friends,
some skill with words, funds,
historical sense, a musical ear,
a basic working body, an idea.

Past Derby the hedgerows thin.
At Sheffield I felt the light pour in
and old men suddenly garrulous.
But travelling back is a curse.
We're infants intoxicated by the dust
that furs the photos of the past.
Where the railway skirted the Tyne
I wondered which house was mine.

From Edinburgh I came back
along the North Sea coastal track.
A pebbledash council house, a mine,
limestone, socialism, rainbows, rain:
how can you live without this shoal
of earth, this silting of the soul?
At Berwick I sat on a bench and tried
to remember how my parents died.

Because our great taboo is death
life has become a spectral path,
and mourning screams to be let out
of every glazed object, every route
is blocked by a ruin that isn't home.
Sadness sits in the frozen form
of jumbled heirlooms we ritualise
and love with antique dealers' eyes.

I'm tired of hunting. Every week
a new camp and a brief break
and back on the interminable march
to the private castle on the beach.
What better ceremony do we have?
The world happens on the grave
of so much beauty, but the ground
is gouged and distributed to the wind.

Looking for a kingdom by the sea
in Alnmouth I paid for a B&B,
and lay among the shower caps
dreaming of living there perhaps.
This is the way we turn to stone:
glutted on visions of living alone.
I found a private corner by the bar,
read Tennyson, downed a beer.

Later, walking on the sand, I turned
to face the ocean, stood, listened.
The roar of the tide was a mother:
You have nothing left to gather.
The mere fact of your verticality
is enough. Leave this privacy
behind and wander into the future:
remember, love, smash the camera.

And the first haul over. Sun
gel and bodyspray,
a swimming pool
Saturday – and Monday

terror, racking up
wounds. They round
and smooth off
finally and you breathe free.

My wartime is with me.
I sing to you
knowing I will die,
my line in the sand

picketed, I cross over
into the ocean
that many do not
recognise, I am swimming

with grace and rhythmic assertion
I am trying, this matters, this us.

4.

Bonus Tracks

HEIRLOOMS OF THE 1970s: J.G. BALLARD, MARTIN AMIS, MARTIN BAX

When I moved into student accommodation built in 1974 a few months back, the seventies objects I'd been carrying around with me since my sister and I sold our family home a couple of years ago started to seem newly apt. It's mostly my dad's stuff that fills the boxes upon boxes we've gone to great lengths to hang on to, and the seventies was unquestionably my dad's decade. Maybe he was a sixties child in some respects – hedonistic, a Hendrix fan – but most of his musical and literary heirlooms are from the subsequent ten years or so (from circa 1969 to 1981). So there are records by Neu!, Uriah Heep, Pink Floyd, Fairport, Amon Düül II, Velvet Underground, Tangerine Dream, Suicide, old copies of *Melody Maker* and *NME*, and a wonderful signed letter from J.G. Ballard, in which he politely declines to take part in a psychology and science fiction conference my dad convened at Newcastle Poly in 1979.

Surrounding myself with these objects in a Brutalist university building feels apt but also weird. Is this a bizarre, atavistic father-son thing? Am I gravitating toward places and things that recall my dad's PhD years as I enter the same phase out of some instinct of quasi-religious remembrance? Is this what hauntology really is – mourning rituals coming back to bite us in the ass, memory and meaning fighting to get out of inert matter in an age of amnesiac secularism? My generation doesn't so much suffer from a generation gap as from an uncanny over-familiarity with our parents.

Anyway, a few days before Christmas, sorting through psychology textbooks, dust-covered copies of *New Worlds*, and novels by Ursula Le Guin, Richard Brautigan, and Christopher Priest, I lighted on this excellent book, published in 1976:

Perhaps people who were actually alive in the seventies can tell me whether or not this is a well-known text. It's certainly not one I'd heard of, and not one that seems to turn up in received histories of the decade. Some very cursory internet research reveals that Martin Bax was a consultant pediatrician in London (apparently until very recently). However he's much better known for founding *Ambit*, a still flourishing literary/arts journal, which Bax now co-edits with middlebrow-poet-turned-monarchy-apologist Carol Ann Duffy, amongst others. Since *The Hospital Ship* he's written only one more book, 2005's *Love on the Borders*.

This is a shame, because his debut really is a belter. The plot is a simple one. After an apocalyptic disaster the titular ship sails around the planet spreading a gospel of free love that is part hippy ethos, part experimental psychiatry. There are some evocative *Children of Men*-style scenes involving human cruci-fixion, which is taking place on dry land at the behest of an unnamed genocidal organisation. Survivors are rescued and healed with the aid of the ship's sex therapies. Some atrocities are experienced first hand. Relationships burgeon and evolve. That's pretty much it.

Ballard was a friend of Bax's – there's an endorsement of his on the blurb – and his influence is clearly discernible throughout. The other notable presence is William S. Burroughs: the structure of the novel utilises Burroughsian cut-up, largely as a means of incorporating copious borrowings from medical journals and psychoanalytic texts. (In fact, take away the scientific material and you would have a novella of less than 100 pages.)

It's difficult to pinpoint what's so winning about this formula. I think it's partly the effortlessness of the outré aesthetic, the sense that writing an experimental, socially provocative novel was *just something one did* back then. This wasn't, surely, a question of ego or careerism (Bax could presumably have ditched the day job for a glamorous literary career). Rather, people wrote these books out of sheer natural curiosity, out of a basic scientific-imaginative desire to synthesize and to create new creative compounds, new stylistic worlds, new social theorems. There's a very moving valorisation of capital-L Love as a societal panacea in *The Hospital Ship* that would be utterly unimaginable in the twenty-first century. The book has a standard sci-fi premise, but it's charmingly scrappy, oblique, rough-edged, unprofessional, and, above all, optimistic.

The crucial thing here is context, isn't it? In other words, Bax was clearly the product of an avant-garde with a clear-ish under-lying sense of the whole raison d'être of experimental fiction. *The Hospital Ship* reads like the product of a very seventies milieu, a counterculture entering its final phase, one that had Ballard, music, experimentation, sex, and science at its centre, one that, for all its flaws, often managed to enlist these things in the service of an unequivocally progressive and even slightly sentimental (from today's vantage point) aesthetic-ethical vision. This world is vaguely familiar to me, the eighties kid, because it's invariably what I think of when I think about my dad the psychologist, the omnivorous reader, the purchaser of willfully obscure records.

* * *

If you want an illustration of how important milieu (or a lack of it) can be to an artist, take the example of Martin Amis. Now, I'm a diehard Amis-hater, but I picked up a copy of *Success* (1977) on holiday last year, and I have to say, it was pretty good. But then, we should remember that Amis was, throughout the seventies, a part of (or at least on the peripheral fringes of) the same counter-cultural milieu populated by figures like Ballard and Bax. This was where early Amis derived almost all of his fictional energy from, and you can clearly see the negative effect on his writing of his gradual estrangement from this environment as he enters the eighties and begins his journey from the Webbite soft-left through the neoliberal centre to the Bushite neo-con right.

In *Success*, however, Amis still seems to have a tendentious grasp of the fact that, in order to write blackly satirical, neo-Dostoyevskyian fiction, you probably have to have some sort of fundamental sympathy for the cultural margins, a basic sense of antipathy to the liberal establishment and the metropolitan literary set (even as you drink/shag/play tennis with its doyens in your off-hours). When you lose sight of this context, you really are fucked creatively. I read *The Rachel Papers* (1973) years ago, and I remember it as a work of ebullient, Chattertonian anarchy; it wasn't experimental or avant-garde by a long stretch, but it was informed by a sort of dark, youthful malevolence (like much of the best rock music of the period, I suppose). This angry-young-man-meets-Pynchon mode seems to reach a delicious urban-gothic peak with *Success*, but by the time of *Money* (1984), which rehashes *Success*'s themes, Amis's focus on excess and deviousness has already begun to tip into over self-indulgence and narcissism (but without the knowing bathos that had previously made these qualities work in situ). All the instruments agree: *Money* is the literary equivalent of a bloated mid-eighties guitar solo.

Again, maybe there's a personal context for all this. Perhaps I'm viewing Amis's pre-eighties oeuvre in a slightly forgiving light because, there on the epigraph page of my dad's 1977 psychology PhD thesis is a quotation from Amis's *Dead Babies* (1975):

I don't know much about science, but I know what I like.

Somewhere in these fragments, I'm certain, is a positive seventies legacy that must be revisited properly before it can be safely laid to rest.

THE WORLD IS STILL WAITING: THE SIGNIFICANCE OF THE STONE ROSES REUNION

Like Brutalist architecture, or glasnost, or Gazza, The Stone Roses are a late-twentieth century phenomenon about which nobody can agree. Something of a joke in their early, hair-gel-and-Blue-Öyster-Cult phase, the Roses leapt quickly to dizzying heights of fame and influence in 1989-90, only to become a subject of mockery once again as their star imploded in the mid-nineties. In the years since, the pendulum has continued to swing violently in opposing directions. In Manchester the Roses are alternately lionised as folk heroes and lambasted for their part in the heritage industry that has calcified around the city's indie music legacy (see FUC 51, a collective blog of "Madchester deniers", for a gleefully scything recent critique of the Manchester Music Museum).

Now, as the Roses reformation is finally upon us, we can expect more of the same. Initial reactions to the reunion gigs have been positive; but the old grumbles – the accusations of musical conservatism, the gripes about "laddism", the compulsion to find new animal-metaphors for Ian Brown's voice – are surely imminent.

Amid the partisanship of the pros and the contras, a bit of critical perspective is needed. The Roses are probably not going to pull off the Third Coming many have yearned for over two decades of hurt. They are probably not going to finally conquer America. They are unlikely, I'm afraid to say it, to produce another really first-rate album (though they may still have a couple of interesting singles in them). Their utopianism has been too cankered by bitterness and infighting over the years, their once Olympian energy tempered by the attrition of age and experience. Above all, they will have to reckon with the toxic atmosphere of the nostalgia circuit they are venturing into, an environment that threatens to vitiate and trivialise every single meaningful thing they have ever done or try to do now. A recent piece for *The Observer* by Miranda Sawyer attempted to filter the legacy of the Roses through the wistful retrospectives of JD Sports brand consultants, and celebrated their contribution to the corporate "Adidas-shod utopia" of post-regeneration Manchester.

But if we look hard enough we might just be able to see something very valuable indeed in the message the Roses are returning to the table this summer. For liberals like Sawyer, the reunion is a nostalgic lifestyle fantasy. For cynics and right-wingers, it can be explained away as a case of greed and rational self-interest finally winning out after years of conscientious refusals to sell-out. But these explanations say more about our own very historically specific form of unbelief and paralysis in the face of Capital than anything else. At the reunion press conference last October, Ian Brown revealed that the band had wanted to make the announcement the day after the riots. He then proceeded to reduce a *Daily Mail* reporter to a puddle of slop with the sort of route-one political invective not heard in British pop discourse since circa 2001: "What does it feel like to support the newspaper that supported Adolf Hitler? That supports the banker cabals that are ruining the world?" Shouldn't this tip us off to the fact that something other than middle-aged revivalism is at play here?

The Roses' resurrection might actually amount to something worthwhile because it offers the prospect of a return to – or at least a reminder of – a tradition of popular radicalism in British music that was to a large extent suppressed in the nineties and noughties. The symbolic death of the Roses in the mid-nineties was a tragedy from which leftfield British pop has never quite recovered; revisiting it might provide some much-needed catharsis, as well as a chance to consider why we seem to have been stuck in a loop of ever increasing apathy and retrogressive

inertia ever since the Roses seemed to metamorphose nightmar-
ishly into Britpop also-rans one day in 1994.

The nineties might have unfolded very differently had the
Roses continued to expand on their radical response to
Thatcher's Britain, instead of retreating into cocaine addiction
and all-night *The Song Remains The Same* binges as protracted
legal struggles unpicked their solidarity in the lead-up to *Second
Coming*. As Jon Savage put it in the Britpop documentary *Live
Forever*: "Spike Island was a good feeling: it was a feeling of
space, it was a feeling of freedom after having been locked up by
eleven years of a Conservative government. But what happened
after Spike Island was that The Stone Roses completely fucked it
up. The Roses were the group who were going to break through
and make it. And they didn't, because they lost their nerve."

In fact the entire Stone Roses project might be viewed as an
attempt to avoid a more general "failure of nerve", an all-or-
nothing late-countercultural offensive against Thatcherism that
stitched together all of the most poetic strands of pop history in
an effort to win back the centre-ground from the neoliberal
moneymen and the postmodern ironists. It was not for nothing
that a previous failure of nerve – 1968 and the Paris student riots
– provided a continual point of allusion in the artwork and lyrics
of the Roses' first album. This evocative date acted as the central
metaphor in a wider campaign of historical summary led by the
band's idealistic lead duo John Squire and Ian Brown. Songs
named after Picasso's *Guernica*, Jackson Pollock pastiches,
Muhammad Ali poses, Situationist rhetoric, Cymande samples,
neo-punk polemics against the monarchy: the Roses knew
popular culture and the twentieth-century avant-garde inside
out, and they pasted it together to create a potent collage of
artistic populism, one that slotted into a wider feeling in 1989-90
that the punitive eighties might finally provoke a revolutionary
cultural reaction.

Throughout their apprenticeship on the margins of the mid-eighties indie scene, the Roses occupied a classic romantic-radical position from which they made repeated assertions that another dimension was lying dormant, ready to burst into life with the right amount of collective belief and imagination. Magical train rides through rainy cityscapes, hallucinations about bursting into heaven, graffiti scrawled on statues, daydreams about young love, lyrics about searching for the perfect day wrapped around chiming Opal-Fruit guitar lines: this was the druggy landscape of dole culture in the second Thatcher term, a place where fantasy and utopianism offered a trapdoor-escape from post-industrial depression, especially in places like the North where the social defeat had been very real. Countless bands from the Smiths to the Cocteau Twins adopted a similar tone of hermetic idealism during this period. What was remarkable about the Stone Roses though – and the reason, surely, why they are regarded with such quasi-spiritual reverence to this day – is that their romantic assertions about another world being possible suddenly and miraculously started to seem realisable as the end of the eighties loomed.

As they approached their peak, the Roses encapsulated a feeling of coming into the sun, a feeling of imminent outbreak and possibility that has very few parallels in the last quarter-century. Often caricatured as working-class boors, the Roses were in fact one of the most lyrically articulate bands in the history of pop. Commenting on "Made of Stone" in an interview in early 1989, for example, John Squire memorably said that it was "about making a wish and watching it happen. Like scoring a goal in a Cup final, on a Harley Electra Glide, dressed as Spiderman". Their lyrics of the time were lacquered with a similar sense of expectant wish-fulfilment, a sense of arrival at a make-or-break historical moment: "I can hear the earth begin to move, I hear my needle hit the groove", "soon to be put to the test, to be whipped by the winds of the west", "you've found what the world is waiting for, I guess it's time", "take a look around there's something happening", "the time has come to shoot you down". The Roses belated renaissance of sixties idealism was something more than the vintage rehash we've become used to in subsequent years. This was an early, sublimated version of retromania: a British reprisal of psychedelia, funk, and 1968 that briefly looked like it might actually amount to something socio-culturally meaningful.

For some, this sort of idealism is always doomed to failure. But the gap between failure and success can be slight. Sometimes a great swathe of society invests a large portion of its emotional energy in a cultural avatar, a vanguard team that embodies the hopes and dreams of a much bigger demographic. The Stone Roses were not alone in symbolising an outpouring of collectivism and radical hedonism at the tail-end of the eighties: the various representatives of acid house, hip-hop, and the rock underground were more influential in practical and global terms than the Roses' and their short-lived campaign of dance-pop tribalism. But the failure of the Roses in the early-nineties – which was basically an arbitrary collision of bad luck and personal fall-outs – was the kind of unfortunate collapse that has profoundly negative repercussions throughout an entire stratum of the culture.

Instead of being a wild anomaly that stood at the summit of a creative apotheosis only ever partially recaptured after the mid-nineties comeback, "Fools Gold" might have been the foundation text of an alternative Britpop: a politically engaged mainstream movement that would never have gotten into bed with Blair, a revival rather than an attenuation of the post-war New Left, guitar pop more in thrall to Bootsy Collins than the Beatles, a progressive filter for – rather than a reaction against – the most thrilling leftfield developments of the nineties from Tricky through Timbaland. As it was, the independent scene crossed over to the darkside and instantaneously lost its whole raison d'être, while the underground progressively retreated into microcosmic obscurity in an age of internet atomisation (cf. chillwave).

It goes without saying that the political and music industry establishment is perfectly comfortable with this bifurcation of pop music – into corporate traditionalism on the one hand and bedroom individualism on the other. What it is really worried about, and what it is just possible the Stone Roses reunion might remind us of, is the sort of significant minority avant-garde incursion that is somehow able to retain an ethos of subversion and an aesthetic of creative openness, whilst also managing to communicate these values to a wide enough portion of the population with powerful musical immediacy.

What the Camerons and the Cleggs and the Cowells and the monarchists and the *Mail*-readers and the Mumford & Sons minions are really scared of is a *normative radicalism*, the sort of aberrant culture that does all the traditional things like make us dance and give us songs to sing at weddings and wakes and school discos and sports occasions, at the same time as it introduces subtle formal innovations and delivers uncompromising messages of insurrection. The Stone Roses Mk. II will have a tough job managing to do anything very effective at all, once Zane Lowe and the Shockwaves *NME* start winding up the hyperbole machine. But if we press the mute button on our cynicism, we might just be able to hear their profoundly optimistic message resounding through a landscape ravaged by a newly virulent strain of Thatcherism at the start of the 2010s: a kind of spiritualised socialism framed as a funky, communitarian song; an angry, affirmative voice promising that he won't rest until Elizabeth II has lost her throne. Take a look around, there's something happening. It's the Britpop that never was. And right in the nick of time.

NOT SIMPLY FOR THOSE MOMENTS' SAKE: A RETROACTIVE MANIFESTO FOR LATE-TWENTIETH-CENTURY POP MUSIC

BEARD

June, 1968. Allen Ginsberg visits Ezra Pound at his Venice home. Pound is old and will not speak; Ginsberg is younger, full of beard, garrulous, enveloped in marijuana smoke. Provoked by silence, or perhaps out of sheer playfulness, Ginsberg plays Pound a series of records by Bob Dylan, Donovan, The Beatles. Pound remains silent, but occasionally taps his cane along with the music. On hearing the lyric *no one was saved* in Eleanor Rigby, he seems to smile, but otherwise maintains total silence.

Nobody knows what this means.

At about the same time, the critic Theodor Adorno writes: "It is uncertain whether art is still possible; whether, with its complete emancipation, it did not sever its own preconditions".

Later, in the eighties, another German critic says: "If one wanted to refute Adorno's approach, one would have to start with his social analysis and prove its results to be inexact by, for example, discussing historico-politically and philosophically another social agency he overlooked; one that would permit progress (and political engagement) to be conceived of".

What an intriguing thought.

TASTE

Here is a picture of James Joyce:

Musically, Joyce's taste was for popular songs. His wife Nora always thought he should have become a singer instead of a writer of ingenious modernist books. Joyce's final work, *Finnegans Wake*, was a book inspired by a popular song.

MOMENT

In the second half of the twentieth century, pop music became the dominant art form of the modernist avant-garde, which had earlier focused its attentions largely on poetry, sculpture, painting, collage, orchestral music, dance, the novel.

This development had been an incredibly long time coming.

For example, in the late-nineteenth century, Walter Pater inserted a powerful aphorism into *The Renaissance*: "All art constantly aspires towards the condition of music". Glossing this notion later in the same study, Pater wrote the following brilliant sentence: "A sudden light transfigures a trivial thing, a weather-vane, a windmill, a winnowing flail, the dust in the barn door: a moment—and the thing has vanished, because it was pure effect; but it leaves a relish behind it, a longing that the accident may happen again."

In the same book, Pater also wrote: "... we are all under sentence of death but with a sort of indefinite reprieve ... we have an interval, and then our place knows us no more. Some spend this interval in listlessness, some in high passions, the wisest, at least among 'the children of this world', in art and song. For our one chance lies in expanding that interval, in getting as many pulsations as possible into the given time ... art comes to you professing frankly to give nothing but the highest quality to your moments as they pass, and simply for those moments' sake."

Even earlier, in a 1795 essay called "On Naïve and Sentimental Poetry", Friedrich Schiller had somewhat pre-empted Pater by saying, "only thus does genius identify itself ... by triumphing over the complications of art by simplicity. It proceeds not by the accepted principles, but by flashes of insight and feeling ..."

Following Pater's crystallization of Romantic theory, most artists in the European tradition fell over themselves for about a hundred years in attempting to establish *an art that was predicated on sudden, pulsating magic moments.*

The aesthetes and symbolists had a go.

Matisse had a go.

The modernist poets definitely had a go:

Sudden in a shaft of sunlight
Even while the dust moves
There rises the hidden laughter
Of children in the foliage
Quick now, here, now, always -
Ridiculous the waste sad time
Stretching before and after.
(T.S. Eliot, "Burnt Norton")

"The 'magic moment' or moment of metamorphosis, bust through
from quotidian into 'divine or permanent world.' Gods, etc."
(Ezra Pound, letter to his father about the scheme of The
Cantos).

GASP

But ultimately, despite continual strenuous attempts, no one
really succeeded in lighting on a suitable *form* for embodying and
containing these magic moments.

Having realized early on that the beauty of art is "a brief gasp
between one cliché and another", Ezra Pound then misguidedly
set about looking for huge, oceanic structures that would provide

a setting for his brief gasps.

That way lay madness.

Similarly, Joyce's youthful obsession with the epiphany resulted in some of his greatest literary achievements. But he too finally succumbed to a kind of silence with *Finnegans Wake*, that vast symphony of sublimely inaudible notes.

How was the "bust through from quotidian" to be achieved, if not by way of massive, semi-incomprehensible artistic schemes? How to find an effective, workable vehicle for the magic moment?

In the end, it happened quite unexpectedly.

IRRUPTIONS

In 1938 Theodor Adorno wrote of pop music (specifically jazz) that "[the tunes] are transformed into a conglomeration of irruptions which are impressed on the listeners by climax and repetition, while the organization of the whole makes no impression whatsoever ... All that is realized is what the spotlight falls on – striking melodic intervals, unsettling modulations, intentional or unintentional mistakes, or whatever condenses itself into a formula by an especially intimate merging of melody and text".

Climax and repetition; unsettling modulations; a conglomeration of irruptions: Adorno might be describing *The Waste Land*!

Like James Joyce, T.S. Eliot was fond of popular music. In the post-World-War-II years, Eliot was in the habit of singing music hall numbers every morning while his young wife Valerie shaved his beard.

Despite this, he probably wouldn't have understood what was so good about, for example, "Jimmy Mack" by Martha and the Vandellas, released in 1967 (just two years after Eliot died),

Yet miraculously, the magic moment has found its ideal home here. *Sudden in a shaft of sunlight ... there rises the hidden laughter of children in the foliage.* The lyric moment—the "hook"—is stated, varied, repeated, bathed in angelic harmony, and then put to bed, all in the space of a perfectly condensed three-minute interval.

A moment—and the thing has vanished, because it was pure effect; but it leaves a relish behind it, a longing that the accident may happen again.

EXAMPLES

Other notable examples of the magic moment at work (chosen at random) include: "Independent Woman Pt. 1" by Destinys Child (2000), "You've Got Everything Now" by The Smiths (1984), "Nuthin But A 'G' Thang" by Dr Dre (1993), "Don't You Want Me" by Human League (1981), "Wuthering Heights" by Kate Bush (1979), "Otis" by The Durutti Column (1989), "Bohemian Rhapsody" by Queen (1975), "Time's Up" by OC (1994), "That's What You Get" by Paramore (2007), "Turn, Turn, Turn" by The Byrds (1965), "Heard it All Before" by Sunshine Anderson (2000), "Two Months Off" by Underworld (2002), "Suspect Device by Stiff Little Fingers" (1978), "And Your Bird Can Sing" by The Beatles (1966), "Babies" by Pulp (1992), "Hang With Me" by Robyn (2010), "I Second That Emotion" by Smokey Robinson and The Miracles (1967), "There's a Moon Out Tonight" by The Capris (1958), "Live Forever" by Oasis (1994), "One Thing" by Amerie (2005), and "Stillness is the Move" by Dirty Projectors (2009).

I've never liked "Teenage Kicks" by The Undertones (1978), but I feel certain that this was the most sacred magic moment known to the BBC disc jockey John Peel, and that this was why he wept whenever he heard it.

ETHOS

Perhaps Adorno was wrong. Like the majority of his coevals, he couldn't recognise that pop music was not, or not merely, a capitalistic diminution of the modernist project. In fact, it now seems scarcely disputable that the pop music of the late-twentieth century was *the ultimate popular realisation of the modernist avant-garde.*

What do we mean by "modernist avant-garde"?

In concentrating on the magic moment we have highlighted the formalist aspect of pop. This was necessary to show that, far from being a phenomenon characterized by banality and dystopia, the pop song is in fact a sophisticated culmination of the entire history of Western civilisation. That is to say, it is by far the greatest art form we have.

But form is never enough.

We now know this, because, while it is still possible to find countless magic moments scattered across the culture, it is much more difficult to locate even small-scale tendencies dedicated to the *organisation* of human beings behind these utopian fragments.

In other words, we have an aesthetic, but no ethos.

DEBATE

There has in fact been a large amount of debate about the terms "modernist" and "avant-garde". In the eighties, Peter Bürger pointed out (probably rightly) that "modernism" should really denote a straight continuation of late-nineteenth century romanticism and aestheticism. Meanwhile, the term "avant-garde" should be used to denote a specific twentieth century tendency dedicated to praxis and engagement with the quotidian (eg. Dada, situationism, etc).

As another critic summarises Bürger's argument, in modernist art experience is "reduced to a mere idiosyncratic feeling of emotional intensity", one in which the particular "materializes momentarily and is never tied to anything". In contrast, in avant-garde art, "the aesthetic fragment functions very differently than the organic whole of romantic artwork, for it challenges its recipient to make it an integrated part of his or her reality and to relate it to sensuous material experience."

Bürger says: avant-garde artists do not isolate themselves, but "reintegrate their art into life".

Pop music, which sent the magic moment into every home in the world, and frequently snuck a countercultural ethos into the admixture, was a synthesis of the two strands. Pop music was formally brilliant, but it was also wildly successful on an organizational level, with its cabalistic movements (psychedelia, post-punk, hip-hop, acid house), its situationist spectacles (the gig/happening, the rave, the music video), its culture of anti-conservative political radicalism, and its exploitation of the *Gesamtkunstwerk* potential of late-capitalist consumerist artefacts.

Late-twentieth-century pop music had the magic moment, but crucially, it was also underwritten by a *democratic, subversive, integrationist ethos.*

"Modernist avant-garde", then, is certainly a fitting appellation for late-twentieth-century pop music.

EPICENTRES

In 1953 the French Lettrist/Situationist Ivan Chtcheglov wrote *Formulaire pour un urbanisme nouveau.*

In it, he argued that Old World majesty and the assurances of organic order are unattainable in the modern world:

> And you, forgotten, your memories ravaged by all the consternations of two hemispheres, stranded in the Red Cellars of Pali-Kao, without music and without geography, no longer setting out for the hacienda where the roots think of the child and *where the wine is finished off with fables from an old almanac.* That's all over. You'll never see the hacienda. It doesn't exist.

Chtcheglov argues that we will never again see the idyll embodied in the trope of the Spanish conquistador estate, the Hacienda. As a result, Chtcheglov argues, we must seek out utopia for ourselves through praxis and collective endeavour. As Chtcheglov puts it: *"The Hacienda must be built".*

In 1982, the idealistic independent pop music label Factory Records actually built a nightclub called The Haçienda, in Manchester. By the late eighties, it had become one of the major epicentres of a great flourishing of electronic dance music and rave culture.

It has since been turned into a luxury apartment building.

REMAINS

Adorno was wrong then. But perhaps latterly he has been proved right.

In organisational terms, pop music is drastically unwell. The worthwhile modernist avant-garde stuff currently being produced (and there remains much of this) lacks the sort of collective architecture previously provided by countercultural institutions like John Peel, the intelligent music press, a vigorous dance music culture, the independent record label movement.

In short, it is now difficult to speak of pop music having a discernible *common culture*, to borrow a favourite phrase of Raymond Williams.

As Greil Marcus commented on the situation in 1975:

We fight our way through the massed and levelled collective taste of the Top 40, just looking for a little something we can call our own. But when we find it and jam the radio to hear it again it isn't just ours – it is a link to thousands of others who are sharing it with us. As a matter of a single song this might mean very little; as culture, as a way of life, you can't beat it.

But sadly, in an age of internet atomism, this kind of shared experience is no longer possible.

What is perhaps worse, the remnants of the pop avant-garde have been diluted and travestied by a cult of retroism which appropriates their face values in the service of consumer fetishism. Pastiche-worship and blithe cynicism abound. The oppositional energies of a potentially alternative culture are tempered and nullified by irony and economic rationalism. The O2 Academy is established as an outpost of corporate assimilation in every town. What now passes for "independent" music in contemporary Britain is in fact its diametric opposite: a professionalised leisure industry for the moneyed upper-middle classes.

In the sixties, Adorno said:

An organization is forced into independence by self-preservation; at the same time this establishment of independence leads to alienation from its purposes and from the people of whom it is composed. Finally – in order to be able to pursue its goals appropriately – it enters into a contradiction with them.

What an accurate summary.

CHILDREN
Wherever there are children, anything is possible.

It is tempting to merely take Adorno's wrongness about the death of art in the mid-twentieth century as a sign that we ourselves are merely blinded by pessimism, unable to see the ground shifting under our feet.

Undoubtedly, there are scattered forms of modernism out there already flourishing or in the early stages of development, waiting to be shaped into humane, progressive formulations.

But the avant-garde teaches us that *we must actively make it so.*

We have our beautiful fragments. But right now we are in dire need of *social structures* to contain them. Art will only remain possible in the future if we come together collectively to build the alternative structures that will safeguard pop's earth-upending epiphanies. We must innovate *society* before we can innovate art.

"I agree", said Ezra Pound, tapping his cane.

Notes

Thanks to the editors of *3:AM*, *Oxford Poetry*, *The Oxonian Review*, and *North-East Passage*, where earlier versions of many of these poems appeared.

"Winning". For Joe Kennedy.

"The Dominican Friars Come to England". Cf. Peter Ackroyd, *The History of England, Vol. 1: Foundation* (London: Macmillan, 2011), pp. 187-8.

"Remembrance Days". Cf. John Cage, *Silence* (London" Calder and Boyas, 1968), p. 73: "We are on the point of being in a cultural situation without having made any special effort to get into one."

"Pantisocracy". For Jon Day.

"The Exile of Delia Derbyshire". The setting here is the farmhouse of the Chinese artist Li Yuan-chia at Banks on the far north-eastern edge of Cumbria. It was the workshop of the pioneering electronic musician Delia Derbyshire for some years in the 1970s.

"The Last Bhundu Boy". Cf. the *Daily Record*'s interview-feature with Rise Kagona, 25 Nov, 2012 (available online).

"On the Proposed Renaming of St James's Park". Cf. the popular Geordie joke.

"On the Footbridge over the A12 at Leytonstone". Cf. Wordsworth's "Upon Westminster Bridge".

"▶ II". Cf. Ezra Pound, *Selected Prose* (New York: New Directions, 1973), p. 70: "The essence of religion is the present tense." The HC2 form will be familiar to many frequenters of British dentists.

"British Poetry 2010s". I have written an elegy for myself, tbh.

"New York Poems". Dedicated to the memory of Adam Yauch (1964-2012).

"The Beehive". For Owen Hatherley.

"The Dance". For Iona Niven.

"Heirlooms of the 1970s". Originally published on the blog *And What Will Be Left of Them …*, 22 March 2011.

"The World is Still Waiting". Originally published in *The Quietus*, 29 May, 2012.

"Not Simply for Those Moments' Sake". Originally published in *Wave Composition*, 5 June, 2011.

Contemporary culture has eliminated both the concept of the public and the figure of the intellectual. Former public spaces – both physical and cultural – are now either derelict or colonized by advertising. A cretinous anti-intellectualism presides, cheerled by expensively educated hacks in the pay of multinational corporations who reassure their bored readers that there is no need to rouse themselves from their interpassive stupor. The informal censorship internalized and propagated by the cultural workers of late capitalism generates a banal conformity that the propaganda chiefs of Stalinism could only ever have dreamt of imposing. Zer0 Books knows that another kind of discourse – intellectual without being academic, popular without being populist – is not only possible: it is already flourishing, in the regions beyond the striplit malls of so-called mass media and the neurotically bureaucratic halls of the academy. Zer0 is committed to the idea of publishing as a making public of the intellectual. It is convinced that in the unthinking, blandly consensual culture in which we live, critical and engaged theoretical reflection is more important than ever before.